Secret Corners 1

A challenge to track down selected 'corners' of Bradford on Avon, Wiltshire.

William D. Newland

Secret Corners 1
First published in Great Britain by FortySix Design, January 2000
Copyright © FortySix Design 2000
Bradford on Avon. UK BA15 1NS
e-mail: 106115.522@compuserve.com

ISBN 0 9537553 0 4

Font: Baskerville
Printed and bound by Cromwell Press, Trowbridge, Wiltshire

Cover photograph: The Town Bridge and The Three Gables
Back cover: The Chantry Boathouse.

All rights reserved. No part of this publication may be reproduced, stored in a retrieval system, or transmitted in any form or by any means, electronic, mechanical, photocopying or otherwise without the prior permission of the publishers.

This book is sold subject to the condition that it shall not, by way of trade or otherwise, be lent, re-sold, hired out or otherwise circulated without the publisher's prior consent in any form of binding or cover other than that in which it is published and without a similar condition including this.

Introduction

Can YOU discover the location of each of the photos in this book? How observant are you? How much do you look up...or down, when you wander through the streets and byways of this beautiful place? Are you aware of the many secret corners that can be discovered?

The challenge: Identify the location of the photographs in this book correctly, and you could win £2,000 (see page 95). Thereafter, you can enjoy the book as a unique souvenir of Bradford on Avon - *with a difference.*

The places photographed can all be found within the Town Boundary - approximately two miles from the Town Bridge. Tracking these treasures may take some time, so whilst some will be quickly identified, others will take considerable detective-work. The task is not as easy as you might think, so get started... now!

About the Author

William D Newland was born in Malindi, Kenya, in 1948 and has lived in Bradford on Avon for many years. He recently worked as a Civil Servant in Bath until he took early retirement in the mid 1990s.

He is a keen photographer, collector of butterflies, and can occasionally be seen fishing on the lower stretches of The Avon. William's hobbies are landscape painting and model railways and he has an extensive track (Double '0' gauge) in his farmhouse attic where he 'escapes' for many hours.

He met and married his wife, Ann, in Africa, before moving to West Wiltshire to start a professional photography business. He has a son and three daughters - and sometimes feels like King Lear.

To my wife and family

Photo 01

Photo 02

Photo 03

Photo 04

Photo 05

Photo 06

Photo 07

Photo 08

Photo 09

Photo 10

Photo 11

Photo 12

Photo 13

Photo 14

Photo 15

Photo 16

Photo 17

Photo 18

Photo 19

Photo 20

Photos: above 21; below: 22

Photo 23

Photo 24

Photos: From left 25; 26; 27

Photo 28

Photo 29

Photo 30

Photo 31

Photo 32

Photo 33

Photo 34

Photo 35

Photo 36

Photo 37

Photo 38

Photos: Left 39; right 40

Photo 41

Photo 42

Photo 43

Photo 44

Photo 45

Photo 46

Photo 47

Photo 48

Photo 49

Photo 50

Photo 51

Photo 52

Photo 53

Photo 54

Photos: Left 55; right 56

Photo 57

Photo 58

Photo 59

Photo 60

Photo 61

Photo 62

Photo 63

Photo 64

Photo 65

Photos: Left 66; right 67

Photo 68

Photo 69

Photo 70

Photo 71

Photo 72

Photo 73

Photo 74

Photo 75

Photo 76

Photo 77

Photos: Clockwise from top left 78; 79; 80; 81

Photo 82

Photo 83

Photos: Left 84; right 85

Photo 86

Photo 87

Photo 88

Photo 89

Photos Clockwise from left: 90; 91; 92

Photo 93

Photo 94

Photo 95

Photo 96

Photo 97

Photo 98

Photo 99

Photo 100

Jottings

The £2,000 Competition

All entries should be sent to "Secret Corners 1", PO Box 2727, Bradford on Avon, Wilts., BA15 1XJ by not later than midnight on 31 December, 2000. There is no age-limit to those entering the competition. You may submit as many entries as you choose, provided they are on the red printed entry form supplied with this book. If there is insufficient space for some of your answers, you may annotate them and attach an additional page with further information for those particular answers. No copies or photocopies of the entry form will be accepted, and once received, they cannot be returned for amendment. In the event of there being no totally correct entry, four separate prizes of £1,000 £600, £300 and £100 will be awarded to the four entries with the highest number of correct answers. So if you cannot identify all the photographs, it is worth submitting an incomplete (partial) entry as yours might be one of the highest-scorers. In the event of a tie-break, the judges' decision will be final.

Every photograph was taken from a public place - accessible to all. They were taken in the second half of 1999, and each location can be found within the boundaries of the Town. The photographs have not been altered apart from touching up or cropping them to make interesting shapes. They were all taken with a Nikon F-3001 camera with black/white film, using a 35-200mm lens.

Note: When describing each location, please ensure that your answer is as unambiguous as possible by including, where relevant, such details as a Street or Road name or a house or building name/number, or any other relevant information such as *"South-West view..."* or *"Beside..."*. In some cases it could be advisable to state *from where the photograph was taken*. If there is any doubt about your description of a location, you run the risk of it being adjudicated as an incorrect answer. For this reason, you are advised to make a rough copy of notes prior to completing the entry form. (Please write clearly.) The official entry form for the competition is only supplied with the purchase of this book between the date of publication and 31 December 2000. Thereafter, the competition entry form is not supplied with the book.

The name of the winner(s) will be announced in *The Wiltshire Times* within the first two weeks of 2001 and if you wish to receive a list of the correct answers after that, you should send a stamped, self-addressed envelope to 'Secret Corners 1' c/o FortySix Design, Bradford on Avon, Wilts BA15 1NS (or enclosed with your entry form).

The Author, publisher, adjudicators, sponsors or printers, or any relations of The Author or Publisher, adjudicators, sponsors or printers may not enter the competition. The adjudicators' decision is **FINAL** and The Author or Publisher cannot enter into any correspondence whatsoever regarding the competition or the result.

The Author and Publishers are grateful to the following who have generously given their support to this unique challenge to the people who live in, and those who visit the historic town of Bradford on Avon.

Geoffrey Saxty *The local Estate Agents. St Margarets Street.*
Saxty's provides an excellent residential sales, property letting and a free valuation service - no obligation. Saxty's also offers a property management service by experts, and can arrange insurance for both landlords and tenants. There is also an in-house mortgage advisor who will be pleased to discuss your situation and find exactly the right mortgage for you. Properties are advertised weekly in Bath and West Wiltshire media and also on the internet, www.propertylive.co.uk/gmsaxtyprop

GW & AR Stone (The Mace Store) *Local shopping and Post Office. Winsley Road.*
In 1949 George Stone and his family built a small local store and gradually developed it to be one of Bradford on Avon's most successful convenience stores. Through the following years local residents have seen a steady expansion of both goods and services – including a fine butchery counter, the Lottery, an on-the-premises bakery, video rental, newspaper and milk delivery and, most recently, a sub Post Office. This is a true 'family' store, which in 1959 joined the growing chain of National Mace convenience stores, thereby offering the benefits of supermarket bulk-purchases for the local community.

John's Bikes *The world of cycling - Walcot Street, Bath.*
We are celebrating our 25th anniversary in the year 2000. The brightly coloured and well-lit shop in Walcot Street, Bath, sells all kinds of equipment and accessories, clothing and bicycles for everyone. The staff are all very friendly and extremely helpful, particularly to those new to cycling.

The Fullard Group *A contemporary learning Company, based in Bradford on Avon, Westbury & Winchester.*
Formed in 1994, the Fullard Group provides training and communication services and products. The Company approach is simple but effective: They understand what is required, work in partnership to design an innovative solution, and then deliver it! The consultancy division serves the UK market with instructor-led courses. The Fullard Group has an expanding number of national and international clients using their multimedia training via CD-ROM and Internet www.fullard.co.uk